OPHELIA'S

BOOK OF DAYS

Ophelia and Family

OPHELIA'S

BOOK OF DAYS

MICHELE DURKSON CLISE

A BULFINCH PRESS BOOK
LITTLE, BROWN AND COMPANY

BOSTON . NEW YORK . TORONTO . LONDON

Designed and produced by Marquand Books, Inc.

First United States Edition

ISBN 0-8212-2070-5

Bulfinch Press is an imprint and trademark of
Little, Brown and Company (Inc.)
Published simultaneously in Canada by
Little, Brown & Company (Canada) Limited

PRINTED IN HONG KONG

Ricky and Zenobia

Ophelia B. Clise

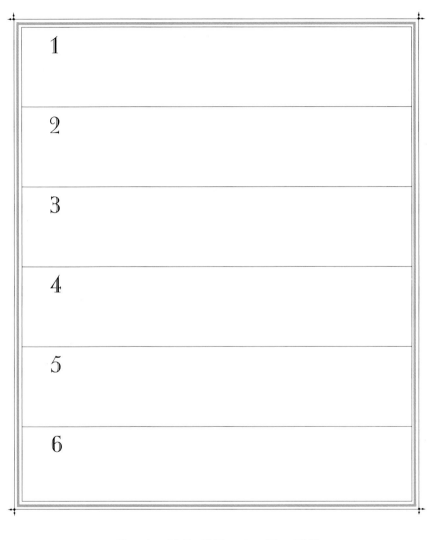

1

2

3

4

5

6

JANUARY

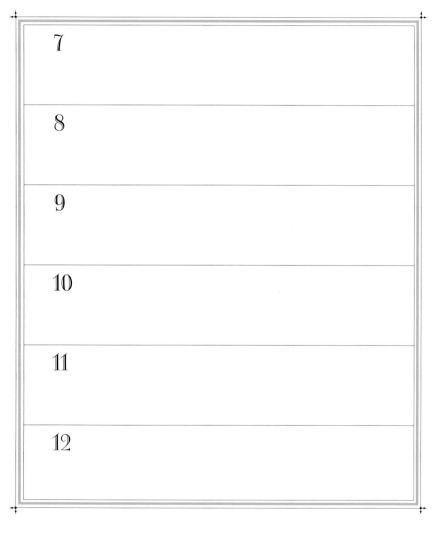

7

8

9

10

11

12

JANUARY

Ophelia with Mr. Ritz

13

14

15

16

17

18

JANUARY

Ricky Jaune with Ratty

19

20

21

22

23

24

JANUARY

Conrad

25

26

27

28

29

30

31

JANUARY

Penelope and Ricky

Clarence

1

2

3

4

5

6

FEBRUARY

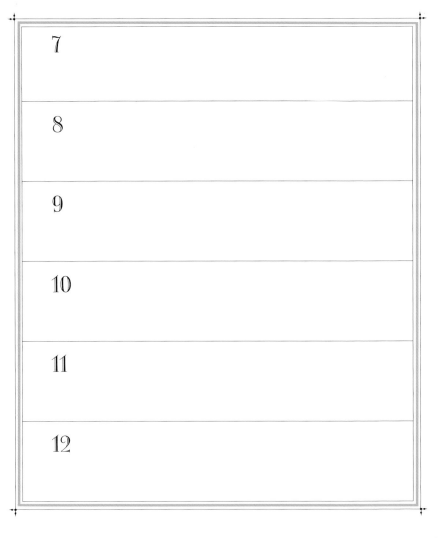

7

8

9

10

11

12

FEBRUARY

Zenobia

13

14

15

16

17

18

FEBRUARY

Schnuffy

Clarence, Ophelia, and Mr. Ritz

19

20

21

22

23

24

FEBRUARY

Dr. Ernest Churchill

25

26

27

28

29

FEBRUARY

1

2

3

4

5

6

MARCH

Ricky and Mr. Ritz with Huckey

In the Conservatory

7

8

9

10

11

12

MARCH

Ophelia at Tea

13

14

15

16

17

18

MARCH

19

20

21

22

23

24

MARCH

Ophelia

Clarence and Friends

25

26

27

28

29

30

31

MARCH

Bedtime for Bears

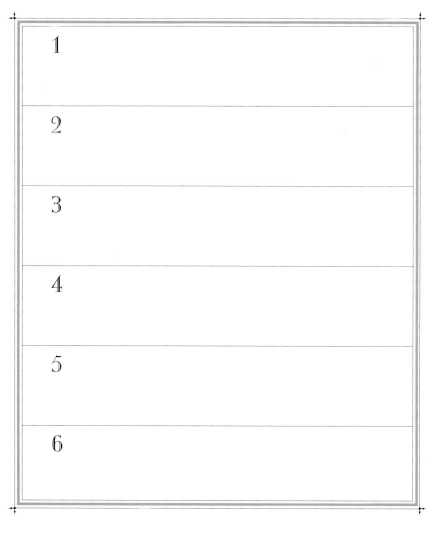

1

2

3

4

5

6

APRIL

Aunt Vita

7

8

9

10

11

12

APRIL

13

14

15

16

17

18

APRIL

Dr. Churchill and Albert with Papillon

19

20

21

22

23

24

APRIL

Ophelia and Friends

Bertie

25

26

27

28

29

30

APRIL

Poli and Aunt Vita with Doggie

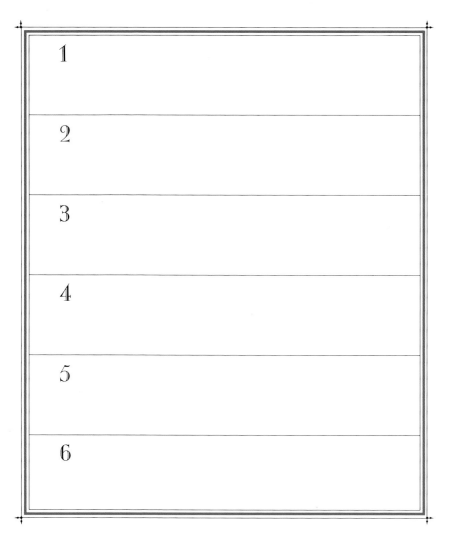

1

2

3

4

5

6

MAY

7

8

9

10

11

12

MAY

Zenobia

Randolph Fielding

13

14

15

16

17

18

MAY

19

20

21

22

23

24

MAY

Ophelia, Aunt Vita, and Dr. Churchill

Ophelia, Mr. Ritz, and Yukiko

25

26

27

28

29

30

31

MAY

1

2

3

4

5

6

JUNE

Golda and Mosche

Popie in Bed

7

8

9

10

11

12

JUNE

Ophelia and Family

13

14

15

16

17

18

JUNE

Schnuffy

19

20

21

22

23

24

JUNE

25	
26	
27	
28	
29	
30	

JUNE

Ophelia and Friends on Way to Picnic

Ricky Jaune

1

2

3

4

5

6

JULY

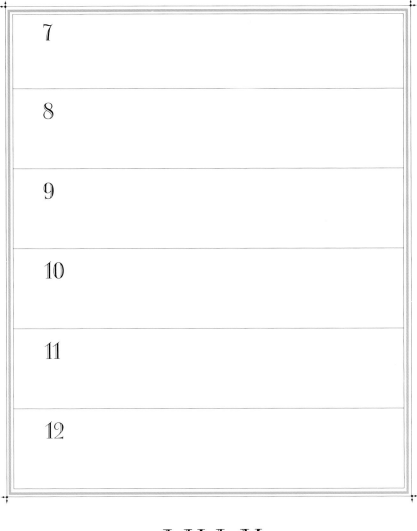

7

8

9

10

11

12

JULY

Poli and Teddy with Mr. Ritz and His
Friends

13

14

15

16

17

18

JULY

Anemone and Albert with Horsie

19

20

21

22

23

24

JULY

Ophelia

Ophelia, Penelope, and Zenobia

25

26

27

28

29

30

31

JULY

Clarence and Crew

1

2

3

4

5

6

AUGUST

On the Road Again

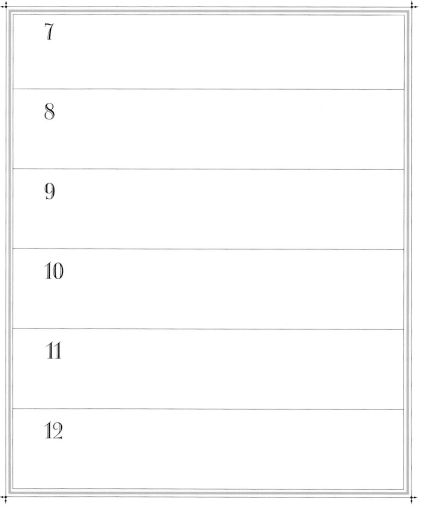

7

8

9

10

11

12

AUGUST

13

14

15

16

17

18

AUGUST

Ricky

Papillon and Aunt Vita with Mr. Ritz

19

20

21

22

23

24

AUGUST

Aunt Vita with the Sniffles

25

26

27

28

29

30

31

AUGUST

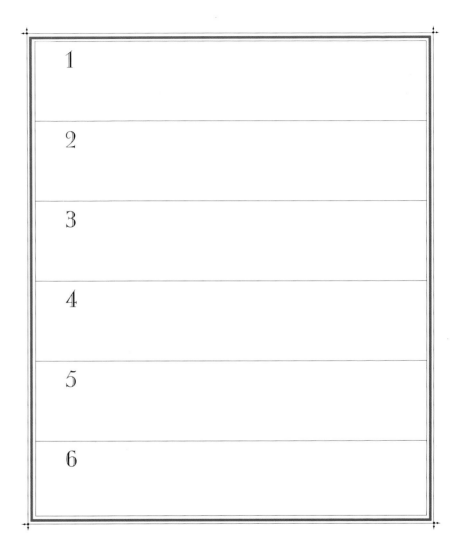

1

2

3

4

5

6

SEPTEMBER

Sophie and Nou Nou with Mr. Ritz

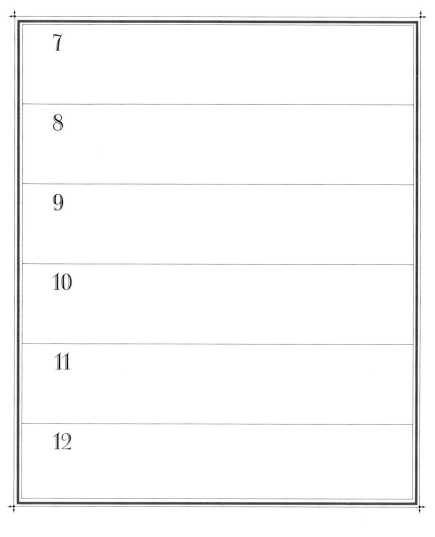

7

8

9

10

11

12

SEPTEMBER

Binkey

Zenobia, Nou Nou, and Pandy

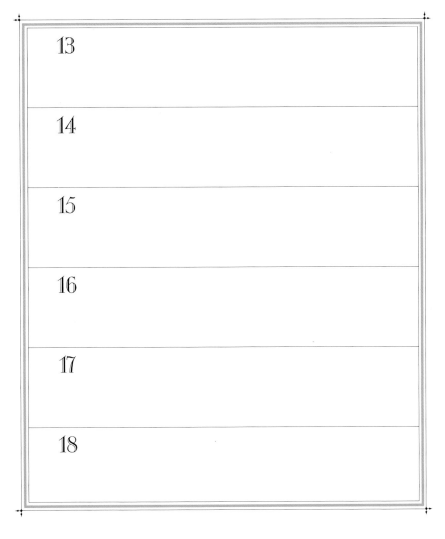

13

14

15

16

17

18

SEPTEMBER

19

20

21

22

23

24

SEPTEMBER

At the Teahouse

Ophelia and Papillon

25

26

27

28

29

30

SEPTEMBER

Zotty

1

2

3

4

5

6

OCTOBER

Happy Birthday

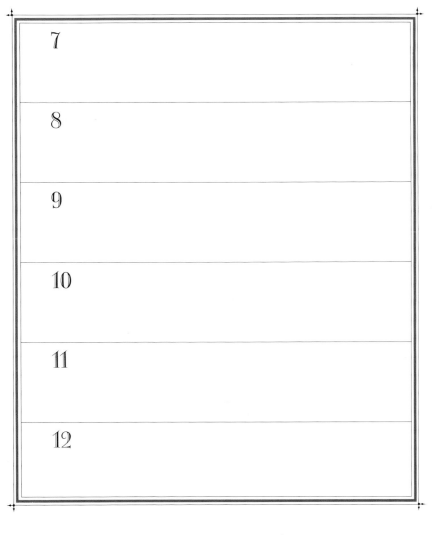

7

8

9

10

11

12

OCTOBER

Clarence

13

14

15

16

17

18

OCTOBER

Nou Nou, Ophelia, and Sophie
with Their Teddies

19

20

21

22

23

24

OCTOBER

25

26

27

28

29

30

31

OCTOBER

Brady Boeing

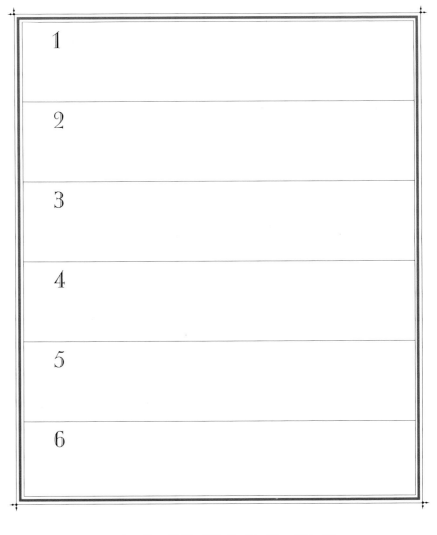

1

2

3

4

5

6

NOVEMBER

Waiting for the Fortune Cookies

7

8

9

10

11

12

NOVEMBER

Ricky, Penelope, Zenobia, and Aunt Vita

13

14

15

16

17

18

NOVEMBER

Dinner Out

Schnuffy and Mona

19

20

21

22

23

24

NOVEMBER

25

26

27

28

29

30

NOVEMBER

Ophelia

Anemone and Albert with Teeny Bears

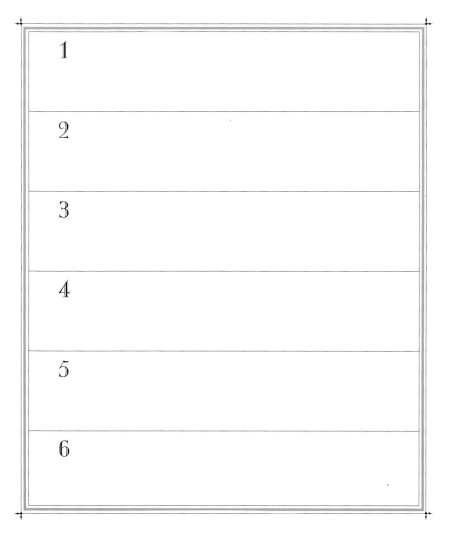

1

2

3

4

5

6

DECEMBER

Schnuffy in Bed

7

8

9

10

11

12

DECEMBER

Ophelia and Sophie with Mr. Ritz

13

14

15

16

17

18

DECEMBER

19

20

21

22

23

24

DECEMBER

Mosche and Golda

Rosario B. Clise

25

26

27

28

29

30

31

DECEMBER